The Coming Day

The Coming Day

Harold J. Recinos

RESOURCE *Publications* • Eugene, Oregon

THE COMING DAY

Copyright © 2019 Harold J. Recinos. All rights reserved. Except for brief quotations in critical publications or reviews, no part of this book may be reproduced in any manner without prior written permission from the publisher. Write: Permissions, Wipf and Stock Publishers, 199 W. 8th Ave., Suite 3, Eugene, OR 97401.

Resource Publications
An Imprint of Wipf and Stock Publishers
199 W. 8th Ave., Suite 3
Eugene, OR 97401

www.wipfandstock.com

PAPERBACK ISBN: 978-1-5326-9637-4
HARDCOVER ISBN: 978-1-5326-9638-1
EBOOK ISBN: 978-1-5326-9639-8

Manufactured in the U.S.A.   11/18/19

"Harold J. Recinos' collection, *The Coming Day*, is filled with poems of great *cariño*, of a sensibility that is attentive to the faces and voices of those forgotten and rendered invisible by systems of oppression and neglect. His indignation at injustice, his loving attentiveness to the least and lowest remind us that we create better communities, countries, selves by the quality of attention we bring to bear on all those who are part of our many circles. His is an abiding and big-hearted imagination."

—Julia Alvarez, author of *In the Time of the Butterflies*

"Harold J. Recinos is the Truth! He is a bona fide voice for those seldom heard: those society ignores, beats back, keeps down, shoves out, erases. *The Coming Day* is a clarion call of compassion and balm for healing that must take place in order for us to advance as a human race. Recinos' poems are stand-ins for searing soul-searching for a world sliding off its axis. These poems are the most necessary nourishment for they do what James Baldwin posits—bear witness! Recinos is a timely poet . . . needed now more than ever."

—Tony Medina, author of *I Am Alfonso Jones* and *Thirteen Ways of Looking at a Black Boy*

"These poems are the stabbing rhythms of a passionate discourse between a culture's fading past and its hopeful future. This lovingly sad and lovingly alive collection teems with Harold Recinos' graceful voice of a street philosopher, a powerful pastor, and a kind professor, while never pulling its punches."

—Ernesto Quiñonez, author of *Bodega Dreams*

"Deeply felt and urgent, *The Coming Day* presents a unique voice that demands to be heard, to be heeded. No one but Harold J. Recinos could have written poems as searing and transformative as these."

—Lorraine M. López, author of *The Darling*

"The poems astutely gathered in *The Coming Day* are so timely and urgent. The taking away of children from mothers, the inhumane conditions at the border, the way the rest of us turn the other cheek—these are great poems of witness and great humanity. Recinos gives voice to so much that remains unspeakable, dark, and disturbing about how people suffer at the hands of governments and politicians. These are immensely important and necessary poems everyone must read."

—**Virgil Suarez**, author of *The Pained Bunting Last Molt* (forthcoming)

"Throughout his distinguished career, Harold J. Recinos has displayed the rare ability to be equally at home in the realm of academic writing and creative writing. It is quite a gift and feat. And so is this: whether operating in the vein of one or the other of these expressive modes, he has always been able to challenge and inspire us all the same with moving words that probe deep and hope big. These powerful poems on a wide variety of themes continue and extend this trend. I highly recommend them to one and all!"

—**Benjamin Valentin**, author of *Theological Cartographies: Mapping the Encounter with God, Humanity, and Christ*

Contents

The Color White | 1
Empire | 3
The Vigil | 5
God Bless America | 7
Protest | 8
Gethsemane | 10
The Altar | 11
Flower Child | 13
Little School Girl | 14
Politics | 16
Cash | 18
Heritage | 19
Beginning | 20
Dream | 21
Ana Maria | 22
The Dictator | 24
I, Cry | 25
Flight | 27
Rising | 28
Alms | 29
La Nena | 30
Remittance | 31
The Psalm | 32
White Visitor | 34
The Park | 35
North | 36
El Paso Bridge | 37
Madrid | 38
The Wanderer | 40
The Fall | 41
Crowded News | 43
Holy Mother | 45

Waiting | 47
Second Coming | 49
Spanish Harlem | 51
Rubble | 53
Woke | 54
The Café | 55
Trickery | 57
Snow Day | 59
Listen | 61
How | 62
Niños | 64
Lost Country | 66
Christchurch | 68
Bind Us | 70
The Disappearance | 71
The Letter | 72
Rice | 74
Confession | 76
Sonia | 77
Yankee Doodle Dandy | 78
El Mercado | 80
Ashes | 81
The Playground | 83
Lost Boy | 85
Saint Patrick's Day | 87
The Pentecostals | 89
Salsa | 91
God | 92
La Plaza | 94
Executive Orders | 96
Graves | 98
Created | 100

What Gospel | 102
Judges | 104
The Buried | 106
Words | 108
El Norte | 109
Street Name | 111
The Walk | 113
Never a Prayer | 115
In These Times | 117
God Knows | 118
The Methodists | 119
Barrio Boy | 120
Good Friday | 122
The Bell Tower | 123
Confess | 124
Dear Friends | 126
Postcards | 128
Easter | 129
Godless | 131
San Juan | 133
The Apartment | 134
The Vacant | 136
Idolatry | 138
The Other Stars | 140
Midnight | 142
Prayer | 144
Waiting | 146
The American Way | 147
Cross the River | 149

Sunrise | 151
Neca | 152
Weep | 154
The Republic | 156
Carmen Julia | 158
Favored | 159
Madness | 161
Subway Station | 162
Forty-Five | 164
Little Sister | 166
Speechless | 168
Brittle | 170
Crossing | 171
Near | 173
Loosened | 174
The Cross | 176
Naked World | 177
The Darkening | 179
Father | 180
Suffering | 182
Little Bird | 183
When | 185
Mentiras | 187
Migrant | 188
Politics | 190
Morning | 191
The Cry | 192
The Anniversary | 193

Acknowledgments

A word of thanks goes to the Center for the Study of Latino/a Christianity and Religions at Southern Methodist University and the Henry Luce Foundation for supporting this project. I also want to thank the people who shared their wisdom, crossed borders, and encouraged me to find the words for each poem. Lastly, a special word of thanks to the people in the barrios and colonias born on God's day off.

The Color White

the journey to a suburban
home in a world of white
belief was the place I went to
weep alone and toss words
like pitched pennies on West
Farms Road. I'd lay awake
trying to recall the scent of
a Puerto Rican kitchen, the
conversations around a red
Formica table with a mother
convinced heaven is a place
populated by dark-skinned,
Spanish-speaking angels and
spics like us were just plain
beautiful. one morning birds
talked loudly at the window,
I heard laughter coming from
heaven and my mother took a
call on a bathroom telephone
from Cynthia the gossip who
lived across the street, I listened
secretly to what was said, then
learned it was more delicate than
whispers in an ear—Ma was
planning to throw away her
boys! I was picked from the
streets by a pastor, lived for
several years with his white
family that caught the drip
of my Puerto Rican tears,
experienced life saved from
a junkie death and had this

pious white man hand me
pages to read from South
American theologians inflamed
by the banquets of the lily-
white West! Damn!!! home
is still a strange feeling but
family love will never stop
being achingly tender for me
in God's world where the
exhausted walk.

Empire

consider the injustice

of those walking the streets

in cities, towns, and tiny

villages who can only see white

faces belonging in this land

that was stolen from murdered

peoples. consider how easily

the foul-mouthed politicians

take the truth out of reason

and use the very air we sniff

for punishment. consider how

many citizens know nothing of

life beneath bridges subjected

to the impeccable terrors of

a pretentious great State led

by an über-thug! then, you

will have a glimpse of life

familiar to undocumented

human beings and fugitive

slaves!

The Vigil

for nearly three years we
have looked upon them in

sadness, the scared bodies
in overcrowded cells, asleep

beneath bridges, pacing the
distance to toddlers' graves,

the darkness gnawing away
their souls. officials never

admitting they are kept like
animals in cages in a deterrence

experiment learned from lessons
in books dating back centuries

that never mentioned a colored
Christ hanging on a cross with

open arms for guiltless prisoners
of the State. for nearly three years

we have seen thinning migrants
raise their truthful cries to the

Lady of Sorrows, watched the
gangsters in leadership fill bags

with rosaries, saint medallions
and more than one crucifix. after

the vigils and listening to elegant
broken-English speeches, we are

certain a mysterious presence will
lure even churches back to truth and

into the company of peasants with
secret hopes and dreams for drawing

the world close!

God Bless America

when they confess "God bless America"
in fancy churches after keeping dark
strangers in cold wire cages, begging
for mercy, and the rich white politicians
keep harmony with a wacky president
tweeting national secrets, they should
expect God out of service. when their
quivering pink lips proclaim they are
merely servants of the almighty way
out in heaven and they seek better days
by unleashing the ambitions of crucifixion
while not shedding a single tear for Brown
human beings prematurely dead in criminal
camps their jaundiced soul paraded in the
daylight is the only thing that sticks in God's
eyes. when they preach ancient truths but read
from a Reverse Standard Version of the holy
Scriptures, declaring hate an argument for
Christ, the stones will speak against them,
the land will unearth bodies and not a single
blessing will issue forth for the goose-steppers
darkening the landscape. when they sing for
divine blessing, they should not be the least
bit surprised when God's Black hand, like a
rare historical intervention, slaps them for
every obscene transgression.

Protest

when they rounded up the kids
held tightly by mothers' hands

beneath a scorching sun with all
your piety you did not protest

enough. when they translated
Spanish names into simple numbers,

confiscated light bags carried for
border-crossing, including pictures

of our disappeared, took children
out of cages to rape, and forced us

to wear reeking soiled clothes for
weeks, you did not protest enough.

when the uniforms carried Brown-
faced toddlers away in boxes made

from cheap wood, tossed their broken
bodies across the border to villages

despaired, and the knotted hearts of
elders threw their clamorous words

north, you did not protest enough.
when we ran away from the soldiers

your country trained, fled the gangs
born on your English-speaking streets,

worked to make your country rich
and hid in shadows dying several times

a day to understand white hate, you
kept silent. when we mention how

your Uncle Sam plunders from sea to
shining sea and right across our border,

question the blasphemy singing God
bless America, you with Sunday choirs

choke us with a little more crooked
Sunday hell.

Gethsemane

in the city that night cannot
make sleep in this country made
from the blood of Indians and
on the heads of slaves, I stood
on a quiet corner trembling with
dreams never licensed for *barrio*
spics like me. Spanglish words
creaked inside my head like an
old carousel playing music with
accents, while the world, laughing
about ghetto life with a big white
face, drove down Westchester
Avenue in a dark blue suburban
with shiny wheels. in the dream
I waited in a silence that did not
speak any language, listened to
the sound of a tambourine exiting
a storefront church where people
prayed for a divine rescue party,
and I thought to myself not even
the cruelest day mixed by elected
barbarous old men and the wicked
packs running with them will keep
people like us from landing upon
the lushest dreams.

The Altar

there was a Bible on the
altar in the bedroom where

the short-boned friends of
mother came sometimes to

kneel. they often read the
texts together taking turns

out loud, staring into each
other's eyes, waiting for any

kind of miracle and new kind
of knowledge other than the

familiar hard times. I watched
their religion pleading in front

of saints, flipping the pages of
a leather-bound Bible, begging

for another day with a full plate
of rice and beans. they smiled

whenever it was time to add a
candle to the tiny shrine to offer

thanks for some little favor and
I suspected if the Lord showed

up the mystery would not prove
greater than the company they

kept. I will never forget how
these women, with their broken

English dreams, spun a new Eden
with their poor lives and how the

religious doctrines priests taught
at their church blew away like

trivial dust.

Flower Child

the tears walk inside me
when the evening news
hour begins and my slow
steps halt to listen. the
words entering the room
declare hope is out of season
and I tremble at the moment
trying to summon justice
from heaven. again there
appears to be no end to
the defiling voices with long
reach, the fascination with
inflicting on the vulnerable
more pain and letting hate
in the name of God run free.
tell me if you please how to
chase away despair and find
truth ripening like fruit to
make us complete?

Little School Girl

the little girl walked down
the steep hill each faintly lit

morning to school, the late
Spring birds already awake

with song, the Cathedral bells
announcing the fresh hour,

her clothing exactly pressed
and the sidewalk hardly ready

for the new day calling her
name. a pigeon's feather

drifted in the air, beckoning
her to the Catholic school a

few more blocks away, miles
from the factory where her

mother worked, distant from
the pale noises downtown

and radiant with the glorious
knowledge of heaven and

earth that would float down
from a mysterious place to

rest in her slight hands. in
the classroom the day began

with a morning prayer that
invoked the name spoken by

the tongues of people around
the world made of every color

on the wandering earth. for
you today, little girl, a thousand

flowers will fall from the sky
to delight your quiet eyes and

make your beautiful Brown
face beam.

Politics

under the bridge that drips
water long after the clouds

have cried over our heads
I will call out your names in

these wretched dark days. I
will write letters to the party

of white sin that once upon
a time saw slaves set free to

denounce the injustice that
you feel, the crimes against

humanity for the sake of the
White House's vain dreams,

and regal banquets underway
in the high-crime places never

bent. I promise to walk in all
the halls of government, visit

in the churches, march down
city streets with tears for you

swelling my eyes, pointing a
finger at the foul politicians

who aim to please impulsive
white hate that hurts and kills

people with dark skin. so long
as I live inside this malicious

history I will not allow truth
to be told leaning on its side,

painted over by brand name
lies and trampled underfoot to

be kept from the citizens' gaze.
when you find sleep tonight

hungry in a cold cage under
the road, huddled in each other's

arms, I will join you to pray
against a brutally violent, white

culture, its philosophers, pastors,
priests, and legislators determined

not to be corrected by a God of
life who weeps with you.

Cash

you carried
three five-dollar
bills, folded up
tiny and stuffed
into a backpack
hidden pocket,
through a less-
loving world
in shoes too
small for your
feet, clothes
donated to your
church by Americans,
and with dreams
enclosed in a
language still
promising lessons
about God.
you stared at
the naked river
in the dark, with
the moon ministering
to the baptized poor,
stepped in, and tried
to say your first broken
English prayer to Jesus
standing on the other
side with a stare.

Heritage

in my Brown skin
the color of earth,
Puerto Rico in my
scarred veins, dark
like the fifth floor
in Tito's building,
older than religion
dishing up forgiveness
like a fast-food meal,
I sat on the stoops of
the mothering block
to learn from Spanish-
speaking tongues the
truths omitted in the
church, schools, and
television screens of
the tropical paradise
America keeps in an
open-air cell. in plain
borrowed white man's
English, my Black soul
will speak differently
until time is done and
my Indian father's Lord
comes!

Beginning

the first light has naturally
appeared.

on the silent earth last night's
animals scatter with names

children alone know.

the trees here last week are
gone, though song birds yet

come in search of them. a
thousand tongues will wake

before clocks strike the working
hours.

shortly, sidewalks will host
languages near and far.

listen!

Dream

she
carried
a dream
like a
precious
stone
across arid
land.

she made
use
of it
in the
language
born
of her
beloved
brown earth.

she held
it like light
in
the dark
to tread
the
Rio Bravo
with
hope
in
a
bulging
belly.

Ana Maria

in a jail cell made for

blameless mothers on

the run, Ana Maria cries

for her child taken by

uniformed men to some

other violent space and

she worries the walk from

her Nazareth with the little

girl will never see the streets

of Bethlehem. among her

things, she keeps a picture

of a sister disappeared two

years earlier in an unnamed

void, and now, nearly blind

with grief in the USA-made

detention stall, Ana Maria fears

news to come one day that her

toddler daughter was carried

out of a wire cage in a plain

pine box. America, America,

the anger when such death

comes will never end.

The Dictator

we saw him once before in
the world blocked of light,
a grotesque swarm of flies
buzzing above his head, busily
dispensing sadness seven days
a week, church altars always
trembling at the sight of him,
the heavenly stars refusing to
call him sire, and blowing out
the candles we light for the
dead. we saw him conspire to
make us blind, offering prayers
with the language of death, luring
his flock to perfect hate and glad
to wear his expensive shoes before
the burning bush. we saw him walk
with the goosestep the nationalists
adore, push a foot down on thin
children's necks, proclaim litanies
of shit for others to praise, drag the
entire country into his unforgiving
game and have counterfeit preachers
declare through him Jesus speaks—isn't
this enough to make us entirely renounce
belief?

I, Cry

I cannot explain why a knot
forms in my throat, why I cry

for my dead brother, grown
children, faded memories of

the Bronx, how dark people
are treated inside America's

border and the dispossessed.
I wish the words came to me

to explain the tears that come
when I look at the spires of

the big church, the children in
careless play in this world too

polarized by hate and youth
drawn away to fight the wars

of greedy old men. I cannot
describe what happens to my

heart when night is detonated
by the screams of USA-made

citizens watching their mothers
dragged away in cuffs in the

small hours of morning and
feeling quite clueless about

who to blame. you will not
believe my tears that say the

place I come from is very much
like Auschwitz and full of Black

and Brown people I cannot
protect—so I cry impatiently

waiting for good news to
come.

Flight

where are the theologians
of resistance for whom truth,
defying the words of cruel
politicians, is more honorable
than good reputations? where are
the bishops who stand up to the
rotten lies of legislators, their
vigorous mockery of law, equality,
and justice? where are the pastors
and priests who denounce the
hate masqueraded as piety by
the head of a goose-marching
State? where are the citizens of
ethical disobedience unhesitant
to call evil policies the clearest
sign of crimes against humanity,
invented for the delight of gleeful
sadists with stone hearts? where
will you be when they come for
those of us who mostly eat corn,
rice, and beans, when our hearts
stop beating as they take our
weeping children, when triumphant
bugles blow to celebrate another
migrant death, when no one is
left to bear witness to the social
creed and American dream so
carefully eclipsed by stone-cold
times? where are the voices from
Abraham's root?

Rising

we are splinters from
heaven, fragments of
divine love, beautiful
and varied dark bodies
made at the beginning
of time by God. we are
the night in the desert
with toddlers afraid, the
eyes watchful of clouds
that rush across borders,
the public square, the market,
the cemeteries, the jails,
and the poor you will see
in the great house beyond
stars. we are the hungry,
the lame, the naked, the sick,
the women, the widows, the
gay, and the unnamed leaving
Christ speechless in church.
we are the ruins of conquest,
the blood on your flag, the
Virgin de Guadalupe, the
tale of climate change and
the loud screams you hear in
your heads, the malls, the raids,
the streets, and inside those fancy
flat-screen TVs. we are the people
too Black, too Brown, too Red, too
Yellow, too weak, too small, and
too poor to be alive say the white-
hooded, loud voices, euphoric
with idiocy—yet we rise on
these forbidden streets!!

Alms

the old woman cannot
go on begging for long.

those hands will go on hurting
though pedestrians drop change.

by the waters of Babylon, she
will sit dark nights to weep.

with nowhere to lay her old head
she will wonder about the light of God.

I listened to her thin voice speak
to countless feelings inside of me.

in the silence of a harsh hour she
indulged heaven with thin prayers.

on that dusty street I then fell to my
knees with her stripped, sore, and

beggar's hand in mine.

La Nena

on the long
walk to public
school one morning,
where Spanish was
not allowed, she found
her voice itching in her
throat, demanding to get
out. it had an old-world
accent, the land before
America and all Spanglish
born. you can hear the suffering
from the working Puerto Rican girls
speaking with their lips, the
mothers once in love who
died, the churches, cemeteries,
Orchard Beach, and her wide
smiling mouth calling us too
without words. on the walk
through her neighborhood in
the company of a warming sun
no one forgets this Bronx girl
created so beautifully Brown
by God.

Remittance

now is a good time to
put together the money
you will send by wire
to the people missing
from your apartment
across the border who
do not dream of leaving
home. you might want
to include a letter about
the cherry blossoms in
the capital you got to see
for the first time, the rites
paraded down the avenue
on floats, the police that
reminded you how fearful
you are of the law and the
many ways you wish your
family was here. I know you
will avoid mentioning progress
is slow, American streets are
not paved in gold, how little
Spanish you speak in public,
the way no one leans forward
to hear what you have to say
about coming North and your
expert slow walk in the fetid
English-speaking world. the
god-blessed money you send
home will keep kids from the
American cage, weary parents
a little more alive and you from
screaming at heaven if even for
just another day.

The Psalm

the strangers who find me
on the corner can talk to me

about their stories of departure,
the wounding experiences that

made their shadows flinch and
what they thought on the dark

nights thick with stars. when the
strangers come to the *barrio* they

will find me in the darkness this
world loves, still weeping for the

infants placed in new-built cages
the songs of heaven never reach.

I am the Puerto Rican junkie with
deeply scarred veins too thick for

your saccharine God's blessing,
the nobody among nobodies of

the *barrio*, the piled rubbish of
the American way, the outsider

the couriers of evil all over this
land call spic, the inventor of hip

hop to explain Shorty's rooftop
OD, the murder of little Julia for

grocery money, and the conga
and timbales africando at the

very center of my beautiful black
heart. when stumbling footsteps

find my sacred corner and tired
Brown migrant feet in search of

a home begin their new day in
this wretched American play, I

will revise the Psalms of
lament with them on every

fucken corner!

White Visitor

years ago, a white visitor who
dared walk South Bronx streets
paused on the broken sidewalk
to talk with Puerto Rican boys
trying to find a chance to live
long enough to tell old man tales.
that afternoon, the street leaked
more teen junkies into the circle
where the white visitor gambled
time with prayer to convince our
hardened youthful hearts God was
not just another myth. not a single
word tripped out of his Ohio
mouth though none smiled in
Spanglish as they passed with a
message in letters more complicated
than the local public-school alphabet
we had dutifully learned. the white
visitor's words insisted surer than
death smiling at us in a ditch that
more life is to come! on that hot
New York City day we found God
extravagantly making noises against
the tainted reality that whiteness set
loose against Black, Brown, Yellow
and Red people—what a strange
day the white visitor with prayer
delivered, making us stagger on
the way to condemn!

The Park

the voices around me
at midday shouted in
the park where children
chased birds, branches
fell from trees and the
earth in dozens of ways
remembered to go on. I
felt the sweet tug of the
passing time, the leaden
prayers on the park hillside
offered by people who have
for too long lived in a filthy
garden. I stared at the radiant
blue sky, declining to believe
hope was impossibly far from
the hundreds of little clarities
we seek. you see, the truth I
seek is not the faces behind
the razor wire, instead I want to
find it with them in our deepest
and most cherished dreams.

North

in the hallway you can hear
the muffled barking of a dog
coming from the third floor,
the halting footsteps of new
migrants to these New York
Spanglish streets, and the tiny,
sacred, Brown feet that belong
to Spanish-speaking children.
they stared down the dark days
coming last week by the border
fence, turned their faces north
and followed the shivering birds
across the boundary in search of
a quiet spot to reminisce about a
longed-for home. the miraculous
warming sun and silver-freckled
dark sky will welcome them young
and old without papers, the puppet
officials in high office will want to
toss them bitter bread, and before
the nation is drained of color the
defenders of the weak in the name
of God will give voice to their
tales.

El Paso Bridge

God, remember your children
caged by a white president beneath
a bridge in Spring. Let their river
of Brown tears never carry them
away from your Sunday. God,
tell the hard-hearted why we have
come, let them feel the cries of
the young standing beneath an El
Paso bridge, and when they kneel
to pray have them hear the sound
of our trying chains. God, let us
have tomorrow for our daughters
and sons, keep us a little longer
in the light and paint white faces
in power with shame. God, do not
let them keep delivering our Brown
bodies to wretchedness, and make
those who pray for us to turn into
dust lose their tongues in your fire
of punishment. God, do not let them
disguise evil ways in the pale shade
of things called good and rush to bring
about the rapid fall of those full of
poisonous deeds—God, walk a bit
faster and set us free!

Madrid

the rain fell for two
weeks as if the Iberian

clouds were offering
their very first words.

people with swollen
hands and dark skin

talked with me on the
street corners, in alleys

and cafes about their
struggle-laden lives,

the national sentiments
stacking up against them,

faces red with infinite
scorn ready to devour

strangers from any black
shore. they lived in broken

nations and now could hardly
remember their dreams. Langston

Hughes once met Black humanity
wide awake on the very same

Madrid streets that Franco
shelled, but I listened to my

dark-skinned people say in
flawless Spanish it looks

like white power will never
hand over justice to them.

The Wanderer

tell me tonight,
on this ancient
land that cannot
speak, why you
roam? on this lost
street, beneath an
immense sky close
to Calvary, remind
me what made you
rest here? tell me what
happens when the
cold Iberian wind
blows against your
tearful eyes and black
heart? later, I will pray
slowly with my Spanglish
tongue for the places
you and I have left on
distant lands with crosses
for others to see.

The Fall

it hurts to reach the sixth
grade trapped in an open-

air cage with a needle in
your veins. against these

young bodies white dope
comes like a dreamless

empire creeping into veins
to peddle a heaping stack

of chains. the sacred little
faces with scarred Brown

arms spill their dreams on
rooftops like the spot where

little Papo shot up and fell
off the ledge. the local priest

did not even bother to come
out to cry for the little boy

who had just died in a harsh
Puerto Rican world. it all

happened on a school day,
the newspapers never got his

name and the event was just
another blind sight left to be

carefully swept away to the
cemetery with the wooden

Christ at the front gate. shit,
I still hear the kids weeping

and the young mothers crying
and cursing in the South Bronx.

Crowded News

have you heard the news
this morning, crowded with

migrants taken away and
poor children hiding in the

darkness holding hands? do
you remember how these

people at the edges of American
life who spend each day trying

to find cures with prayer were
written about in the *National*

Geographic subscribed to by
the local public school? don't

you want to see the faraway
camps waiting to receive the

frightened mothers and kids
from US-martyred lands? don't

you want to stand before the
mural beneath the bridge left

there by the *barrio* boys who
crowded last night's Fox lies

and drawn with memories of
hunger, broken bodies, desert

thirst, pastors without tongues,
soldiers standing guard, and

politicians with their backs to
a dark-skinned, crucified God?

I see them limping on the street,
in the near empty shopping malls

with sad faces staring at things
outside of reach, regularly murmuring

about hell unlocked and the
old commandments of the holy

book in houses of bondage easily
set aside.

Holy Mother

the flight came so suddenly
though the gangs and Herod's

thugs who roamed the village
streets of the darkened country

trampled about with harm. she
trembled with an infant in her arms

thinking of the long walk north
and the rumors that an open Bible

would not prevent the border cops
from prying her fingers from the

child. the days of keeping silent
and begging to hear the soft voice

of the Mother of God delivering
a message of salvation withdraw

with each step. she will arrive
with stories of the violence in all

her days, the history of American
war crimes against the helpless of

a nation that did not lift for them
a welcoming light. she will not accept

imprisonment, her infant's name
unspoken, the number designations

to be given, the face of fear in
jail and the mockery the English-

speaking citizens have for the
rescuing blood of Christ. each

night she will kneel down in a
cell with tears for her child, pleading

for heaven's chariot to come to steal
her and the crying innocent away!

Waiting

On Sunday, walking to
church, holding hands

that weighed very little, a
mother looked at her boys

and wept. even then she was
trying to escape the white faces

content to hate, the fear swelling
her Brown skin, the ICE prison

waiting for her with unforgiving
stares and the liberty that took flight

with fucken bruised wings. after
many years in church she still did

not understand why the reputed
good Lord barely listened to the

words oozing from her wounded
soul. the big church sermons left

her completely in the dark and the
colonized faces in the Spanish Mass

kept projecting more hard times.
each tear that rolled down her Brown

face said God was far away. I did
see her about a week ago, waiting

like always for good news to find
her rotten apartment and hungry

boys with a simple knock on the
door.

Second Coming

the last time I heard mention
of your name was in the big-

steeple church from which a
well-dressed white man was

reading from a leather-bound
Bible stories that someone in

your time wrote down never
thinking how one day it would

make money for preachers in
religious business. politicians

like to hear themselves say Jesus
too throwing little bits of what's

left of you to the public that is now
curious about your very exceptional

disappearing act that permits presidents,
bishops, pastors, soldiers, cops, and a

huge lot of unrepentant thugs to
sell out. I am afraid to say your

name is worn out and overrated in a
world where violence smashes innocent

lives, blows out candles in church, and
fails to restrain the rapacious capital

that will deliver earth to death quicker
than anyone will admit. you once

promised to come back so I figure
this is a good time, Christ, to say hurry

to this world you prematurely left and
deliver acts of kindness for a change. but

if the sober truth is you are never going
to return, then get the fuck out of our

heads, so we can spin godless miracles
on mother earth that money rapes before

it's too damn late!

Spanish Harlem

we prayed with truth
taken in the hand, wet

Spanish hearts, people
who cleared the fence,

pastors holding broken
bread and with the old

little gossips from the
church. we talked to the

torturers with stopped
up ears, the cynics with

exquisite laughs and the
lovers of lies with cold

lips who never say anything
of heaven's slant

dreams. the world that
fed on Bible truths faded

many greying years ago
though the kneeling at

base of the wounded tree
is endless. we prayed for

long about history written
backward, the detours at

the border and the truth
written in us shouting its

way out from our scorched
bones in time for the latest

national conference about
an unsociable God.

Rubble

there was a building here
once where these cracked
bricks, splintered wood,
rusty nails, and wrecked
toys lay. the artifacts of
future archaeology for the
spics who were daily cast
away from a world that
said their lives are of no
importance. the winter
frost is preserving the
rubble that in the South
Bronx has seen many years
of darkness. the celestial gods
have overlooked it, the lily-
white people downtown have not
seen it, and neighboring love
never bothered with its world
of bruises, and harm.

Woke

like the first day at
Orchard Beach with
music played to fill
us with magnificent
feelings of belonging.
like the first walk to the
Valencia Bakery to
get yesterday's bread
for free to eat with a
twenty-five-cent butter
stick with Nuyorican lips
that trembled with life. like
the walk to public school
for a first-time pledge for
teachers who only saw
our Brown skin. like the
bright day on the stoop
we realized America is
home. Lord, we are glad
for this moon, sun, air,
earth, and sudden feeling
of peace!

The Café

the air outside was plain cold
and people filled the café with

replies. Olga sat on a corner
stool at the end of the bar, the

salsa was already playing, the
timbalero who never missed a

well-placed beat had ecstasy
coming out of his eyes, yellow

horns played beautifully enough
to make the Puerto Ricans in the

room drop their heavy loads and
white faces nearly turned the color

of earth. in the lyrical atmosphere
of the space with the best lower-

east-side musicians on stage I could
see this would be a good place to

begin a history book of the salsa
age. in the middle of the room,

with rhythms falling from the high
ceiling, dancers magically circled

the floor with delicious widened
feelings that rendered their Brown

souls naked. the voices in the room
with sweet accents had no need for

crass English, good housekeeping
seals, these people of mine who came

from a long line of slaves that broke
their chains were in the room taking

their time dreaming up light!

Trickery

there was a time when
the politicians were not

the first to abandon the
cries from these rooftops

now carried by the wind. but
they are fast asleep in the dark

night coming up with more plans
about nothing while the heavenly

stars watch over us. in these sad
times, we have plenty of knowledge

about the disturbed narcissist in the
White House who signed a bunch

of Bibles one day in Alabama that
GOP apologists just adore. he stays

up nights to smother American life
with a heart too deplorable for the

likes of God. you can just hear over
painful screams his poisonous talk,

presenting lies as truth. you can see his
hateful smile positioned before thousands

of strangers who are sadistically pounded
into the earth. how long until the coming fall,

the prosecution of law and the blunt verdict
of divinity above? how long until ten plagues

descend on the big house of the counterfeit
president and children beaten by his soiled

whip cry, "Free at last, free?"

Snow Day

the last snowfall that closed
the public schools coaxed the

children into the playful streets
and beggars appeared to wander

the avenue a little less bent. maybe
God that day enjoyed the laughter

on the stoops, the light that fell
on vagabonds' faces, and games

drawing strangers near. even the
pigeons found ways to play by

shaking free the dusty snow from
roosts above Spanglish-shouting

faces. the day never felt cold nor
filled with impatience and the Puerto

Rican widows with uneven smiles
paused on streets, ejected for a few

moments from sorrow. we suspected
before night emptied the block not a

soul would doubt heaven neighbored
us while pitching pure snow and rolling

on its side with gentle winds. the flakes
that floated to earth, soared in the air, and

landed unhurriedly to dissolve on fire
escapes will always be a sweet city

lesson that says the world is just
the work of mysterious heaven.

Listen

now in the wet Spring
outside our window the
eyes of God weep on the
black earth. we gaze on
childhood that makes its
appearance here and there
through the sounding rain,
imagining long messages
sent from the thundering
clouds for the blunders of
the nation. we can see the
water falling as it has from
the beginning, pronouncing
a summons to wash ourselves
clean and hear the voices not
speaking the language used
by us to think. you can see the
stones in the fields drenched
by rain nearly drowned and
ready to say a few lines to
strangers on the road—listen!

How

they learned
to love
differently,
like a candle
flame that
dances
in the
dark,
the eyeing
public
denying
them
the
simple wish
of the
open air
and
clutching hands
beneath
the city's
uncountable stars
with
their many
stories
of delicate
flashes of
love.
they learned
choking
back
tears
in a

world
full of
places
to love
with
the simplicity
of a
forbidden
    kiss.

Niños

the
morning
light
is
for the
children
who
do not walk
country fields,
nor rush
along
wooded
trails.
the
city streets
know
where they are
after
the
enormous
night
is settled.
in
the brilliant
day
these kids
dream bigger
than the
church
and
jump higher
than

the tough
steel fences,
while
carrying their
English-
only books.
these
kids, who
walk
and
play
in the same
old clothes,
whose faces
are painted
on
the alley
walls, will
never know
a white-
bread
life.

Lost Country

in the lost country, with
beautiful stone churches,

you can feel so far from
God just sitting in the pews

made from fine wood. outside
these nice showcase places of

piety you can hear whispering
at all hours about how the good

Lord sent the least qualified angel
to roam the earth and drop more

than a few moral hints to a former
reality TV host with a monstrous

tongue who suffers from delusions
of being a great president. I heard

that just last week in the lost country
White House Bible study the Royal

Court chaplains prayed for the rest
of the country to act like nothing's

going on, to pretend like the naked
head of state is wearing one of his

Mexican-made suits, to overlook the
significant body of sins signed into

law by the hand that grabs women
by their genitals and signs Southern

Bibles. last night in the alley, about
two blocks from the cathedral, the

winos debated between sips of a pint
bottle of Midnight Express a simple

truth that suggested why the hell so
many people show up for worship

to hear a greying pastor sing with
a choir the hymns to make the white

hour great, and never once raise a
voice about the weeping caused by

the white men, inspired by the
stochastic terrorist living on

Pennsylvania Avenue, who kill.

Christchurch

the foreigners
crossing the border
are
held in prayer
after
the evening news
reported
they were killed
at once by hatred
fired from a white man's
gun.
today the horrifying
ditch is a great
deal more swollen by
a fresh load of strangers
with the
wrong religion
and
tint of skin
for the young white
murderer
who never could
see
color was created
by God's sun
shining
on him.
when the wailing
turns into silence
and
the world is still down
on its knees

in prayer,
Lord
give some more
thought to
the foul white supremacists
and
have your old sweet chariot
fly low
enough to run
them over
for
goodness sake.

Bind Us

the crowds
have gathered
for several days in
the city squares
and
religious places
and
the view from here is
public sorrow.
the polished prayers
of the Muslim dead are silent
and
the grotesque crime
of the agent of
white supremacy no
cause of alarm for a
president
masterfully practiced
in guiding hands
of
feverish hate
for blessed heaven
to see.
the crowds are
on the open streets clutching
rosaries, prayer rugs,
and
pocket-sized sacred texts
to beg the gods
to make
the white
benediction of violence
stop.

The Disappearance

we are a long way from
the happy valleys of paradise
in this *barrio*.

on the block book knowledge
will find handled merchandise
damaged.

the faces you see on these streets
will make good trivia from high
philosophy.

the people sitting on stoops just
slip past the church and its latest
theologies.

the white heaven preachers
speak about is blown away
by bitter truths.

down here we wonder about the
theologians who like to hear
themselves.

in these parts suffering is an open
house displaying the imperfections
of God.

The Letter

the last few weeks have left
us all with the strong feeling

that the world deserves a lot
better. the churches, fattened

by straight congregants, fouled
up their interpretation of the call

to love, and white supremacists,
listening to a demented God,

went on shooting sprees. words in
a letter never ache after arranging

the alphabet to speak with the voice
of a sorrowing heart, to say a few last

things to freshly dug graves, bullet-
riddled Mosques, two men in love,

two women wed, and kids wasting
away in American-made cages. you

may think it strange for me to speculate
in a simple letter about these things or

why human beings determined to believe
themselves on the right side of history

imaginatively find others to brutally put
down in the name of extraordinary lies. I am

waiting for the day bitter, rich, old men
stop leading unreflective people into yet

another Death Valley with Scripture on their
lips like they know what it means. I would

like to say hope fills me after writing these
words, but it feels more like gravity pushed

me through the clouds after a brief visit to
heaven to walk more on troubled earth.

Rice

the day they made me
kneel on rice it didn't

hurt, rice grains left a
little dent in my knees,

and though it was the
middle of the week, I

imagined rice thrown
at weddings on church

steps. I wondered why
the Catholic God we all

expected would appear
behind a crescent moon

some nights above rooftops
required punishments

to set kids straight. I waited
for an angel to show up to

tell me "Do not be afraid" just
to have the opportunity to

throw a high-pitched scream
to make its white wings

flap. I looked over my left
shoulder, but the only messenger

next to me was an older brother
with light coming out of his

eyes, which I soon realized was
just a bare light bulb shining

above his face and reflecting
off a bucket of tears dripping

from them. before all the
kneeling ended I went into

the bedroom with a dresser
that posed like a religious

altar and whispered to the
ceramic saints something

about how all the castigation
for minor offenses must mean

God has very little need for
Spanglish-speaking kids like

us. I remember the rice kneel
day took place in the South

Bronx the day Kennedy got
elected president—and his

picture made its way to my
mother's bedroom altar next

to San Martin de Porres.

Confession

the world is growing blind,
strolling farther away from

God, racing after false light,
and gruesomely squeezing

life from the poor. no matter
how many Sundays the saved

kneel to pray, the latest obituaries
report the murder of truth to the

unalarmed. by the time divinity
comes with another clever disguise

to save us from the sweet earth
where for so long we failed to right

what makes it sick, we will be too
busy arguing about the darkening

made by wealth and causing us to
trip on freshly dug graves.

Sonia

she married real young in her
Spanish tongue. her Puerto

Rican body was tired of work and
carrying another kid. she looked at

the Bronx, with her round Brown face,
keeping her caged. she thought about

America, where Christ is white and
dressed in fatigues. she hated people

who taught her to feel shame about her
sweet name. she sat on the stoop, watching

the curved street for the cops to crawl
up. she often felt alone in the dark on

an emptying block with memories of
her dead. she knew the apartments that

were filled with kids feeling scared. she
called out to heaven a South Bronx

list of names. then, she died in America
on a rainy day believing hard days would

soon end. at her vigil, a hymn, a prayer,
choice last words and a few friends with

Spanish-speaking tears.

Yankee Doodle Dandy

in elementary school, I learned
to pledge allegiance to the flag

that said, each day, with words
gathered on its white lips, "You

do not belong." at the edge of
the world I saw little Victor

march to a foreign war, waving
the stars and stripes, and now his

elderly mother bawls on every
visit to the Vietnam Memorial.

whenever I think of the pledge, I
mourn for Manolo, who counted

on Americans to say his Spanish
name and recall the Irish girl around

the corner he loved before the war
in Southeast Asia cost him his life.

look across the wide noisy street that has
been home for us from the lily-white

churches with flags, where you sit
to pray, let the print in your school

books swell with our presence, open
your eyes to the light, reject the WTF

piety yelling in your ears, and confess
America is more colorful than you

care to think.

El Mercado

I still hear the voices
shouting in the market-
place beneath the train
rails. they glide about
the room in Spanglish,
slip out the old doors
and float to the highest
rooftops. stuffed with
barrio curiosities on the
edge of the city they yet
haunt me. I still hear the
church bells ringing in
the distance like a big
question mark about us
on these aging streets
touched for more than
a hundred years by our
Puerto Rican hands and
staggering feet. I would
like this to be the day the
God of the poor cries out
from the depths to tell the
Spanglish-speaking people
still brushing the ashes of
their beloved dead from
grandmothers' shoulders
dreams are worth more than
than the stone-cold bruises
the soiled world gives.

Ashes

with ashes placed on
our foreheads signifying

the cross, days of fasting
on the border, knowledge

of the dark cells where youth
and children perish, death

cannot make us afraid and
the violence of those who

scrawl swastikas on pieces
of the long wall will never

prevent our march toward
life. we look up often at the

nightly stars, whispering best
wishes to the white-skinned

people walking behind the
president who would like to

see us die a thousand times
over, saying, "Forgive them, Lord,

they do not know where they
are going." our children who are

tired leave their mark on the
roadside and wear everything

the English-only country did
to them in villages plundered

by power, wretched today with
poverty and proper USA-made

gangs. with these ashes now
invisible on our foreheads, put

there at Mass in a border town,
we press to reach North, unafraid of

the dark, the intense rejection
and the silence of the grave. we

will quietly sit when night closes
its mouth and the moon lights a

way across the border the ancient
desert with many names knows

too well.

The Playground

you should see the playground
with the big Ceiba tree in the

middle of it, where the Brown-
faced children swarm to elect

sides for a round of real foot-
ball. they will play with the

leather-bound orb longer than
the striking clocks and into the

early night when doors begin
to lock and the smiling women

who sell food off carts wheel
away. their dark eyes filled with

Mesoamerican wonder never
fail to surprise you with how

they can even brighten up the
light. it would be untrue to write

happiness today any other way,
to overlook the secrets of tiny

feet running up and down the
dusty field and look the other

way each time the child who
kicks a goal falls down with wild

laughter. these are the children
to keep from bitter weeping and

closer still to the Spanish-beating
hearts that can love deeper than

God who made them will ever
fully know.

Lost Boy

it was past ten at Columbus Circle
when I realized night is filled with

memories, not rescued by God for
the homeless. quietly, I embraced

everything about her in that time
of absence, saw her image in the

currents of wind blowing north on
Broadway and felt more deeply the

longing for home. I sat picturing that
mother would come out of the

IRT subway station, drowning in
tears for a lost boy, bells from a

local church would begin to ring,
and I would embark on the waited-

for journey to the apartment in the
South Bronx to be once again with

the people who did not speak with
English tongues. I sat alone with

the night, misunderstanding how
time changes us. I ached on that

bench, with my eyes stubbornly
on the station exit. you probably

will not believe me but for more
than fifty years I missed this lady

who believed saints settled her
troubles and I cannot stop calling

her mother.

Saint Patrick's Day

who said you live in the
barrio the day you showed

up on Fifth Avenue to see
the Saint Patrick's Day

Parade? was it the excluded
look in your eyes that gave

you away, or how you turned
your head when somebody

yelled, "spic?" did your
jacket with the Puerto Rican

flag on the back say it all
with its hint of the aroma of

green bananas you unloaded
from the truck parked in front

of the 110th Street Bodega? I
bet it was the Spanglish cheers

you tossed to the Brown-skinned
marchers of the fighting 69th that

today is Browner than white and
Irish by adoption. faces laughing,

voices shouting, drums beating,
bagpipes playing, and there you

are saying every tribe in the city
is sucking in its breath like they

just showed up for a block party
in Spanish Harlem. I know you

walked over from Third Avenue
to watch, the street where little

kids already know how to gasp
for air. *Boricua*, I will cross the

parade line to tell *los blanquitos*
what you said one night on the

stoop with bugles blowing from
an old transistor radio: the *barrio*

es dolor, sueño, y vida!

The Pentecostals

they told me at St. John's Chrysostom
Catholic Church one morning while

talking up stories of divinity that the
Pentecostals who choose to pray in a

storefront are different. I listened
sensibly to the view that Rome had

a more direct line to the story of the
empty tomb and the Lord who poured

himself into streets before departing
the world like a common thief. I lived

in a building with a whole bunch of
Pentecostals, but not one appeared to

be on the devil's watch, unlike the
mystery seekers in Mass and living

with reference to another future. they
even heard the slow-ringing bells drag

European melodies across the block each
Easter loud enough to inspire more furious

reading of their Protestant Bibles. one
Sunday morning, in a Boy's Club camp

made possible by the mayor for inner-city
kids, I was leaving a Mass led by a priest

and Pentecostal boys were entering the
same outdoor chapel with a pastor holding

the good book. I heard them read words
from an Old Testament prophet that took me

back to the building on West Farms Road
where the Alleluias shared with neighbors

a repertoire of hollers, *coritos* and *gloria
a Dios* for the block. I can tell you that

is when my sacramental refusal to believe
everything heard in church began and I

started walking with those who plead
for divinity to hold the spill of *barrio*

tears and bring good days into poor
lives.

Salsa

tonight, music plays in
the lower-east-side café
and the trombone forgets
silence. people crowd the
bar's counter with a picture
of my old friend in a cheap
frame against a dim mirror.
the 3rd Street door opens to
add visitors to the room and
wind blows me to your place
of absence. then, the diasporic
salsa band calls us to push back
the rickety chairs to sway and
moan on weary feet. tonight,
bitterness fades like the scraped
knee on a child and the tenements
on the block are nameless. I like
this café, where night is different,
lovers embrace, and poets light the
room with words.

God

the little boy spent the day
alone in the apartment talking

to God, who had a soft voice
with a Spanish accent and was

closer to him than the religious
altar where he sometimes knelt.

he never saw the divine face
though that did not keep him

from rapping away like the
heavenly figure was sitting

on the stoop watching the
bus rush down Westchester

Avenue. the little boy asked
the accented talker with him

in that bolted-shut apartment, "Are
there really no secrets to discover

in life and no big pitted stones
to speak? Are the dead like Tito

almost dust returning one day soon
with news from the other side?" he

assumed there was something for
God to say, but was instead left in

the silence, feeling certain the almighty
forgot the *barrio* poor most of all.

La Plaza

while we
waited in
the town
square for
nothing
to happen
the park
workers
found
the best
shade by
a leafy tree
to cool
themselves.
they laughed
to comfort
their
weary hands,
the patch
of flowers
they planted
that very
morning
widespread
in the
Mesoamerican
sun.
our eyes
fell on the
cathedral's
cupula slanting
to the

left
and a
Bible-thumping
preacher cajoling
a small
crowd to
believe
in his distant,
US-made,
English-speaking
God.

Executive Orders

the executive orders have
rushed out of office like a

body aflame. they thicken
the chains around liberty,

enliven the stiff necks to
leave their footprints on

dark bodies, and make the
pious turn deaf ears to the

shouts that come from the
American deserts, the mouths

crying in the wilderness,
and the Spanish-speaking

shrines scattered on the arid
land along the border and

the many towns where the
unwanted wait for the murder

of kindness to end. executive
orders leave the Oval Office,

issuing divisions of race in the
name of relapsed justice, white

hoods, rotten politics, and the
billionaire crooks! to hell with

the executive orders making
the country blind to the Brown

people shouting, "The president's
fine suit is soiled with the blood

of dead Guatemalan children
and the stench of his own full-

of-shit lies!" truth will multiply
on locked-up Brown tongues,

and beautiful colored kids
will inherit the earth long

before the executive orders
start yellowing on paper left

for the government-issue
shredder.

Graves

one day
the hollering
tongues
will be
choked
by
their own
toxic
words,
and
the criminal
politicians
will sleepwalk
in city sewers
swarming
with rats.
one day
the idiot
puppets
who
followed the
Putin-elected
Bible
hustler in the
White House
will rot in
their own
flesh,
with Spanish
names
etched
on

their
bones
in
graves
too
good for
them.

Created

in the morning the foreign
tongues in this tenement

chatter. each tells a story of
distant shores full of savage

disharmonies that crash on
English-only ears. yesterday

the old Jewish man on the
first floor shouted out to me

"*shalom*," then offered, "It means
'peace.'" I smiled at him on the

way to pick up spices at the
bodega and saw him wipe a

cheek with tears. in the morning
the second floor of the block church

is filled by God's sightseers who
only speak English and whisper

disbelievingly that divinity blew
more difference into the world than

they care with all their piety to
think about. in the morning, when God

East of Eden ringing bells
in my head to escort thee words to

my lips, "the poor only inherit rich men's sins."

Judges

you
turned away
from
the
throbbing
hearts
already
in the pews,
refused
to take
the hand
of those
you said
have
dirty
heads.
you
trespassed
against
a people
with sacred
names
that
kissed
for
the open
eyes of
God.
you
lack
the childish
wonder

about
the
beautiful
things
that make
for love
in a
world
imagined
by divinity
with
more ways
of being
than
you can
boast
to know.
you,
for the
love of
God,
must
learn to
hold your
tongue
when
same-
sex
others
weep
rivers
love.

The Buried

no,
I am afraid to
see more fleeing
faces banished
from the English-
speaking world,
the border made in
the image of hate,
the howling full
of spite, moons
that come and go
never to deliver a
morning of hope.
no,
I am afraid to
see chains for so
much light, Brown
bodies on the road
that never leads to
paradise, the voices
buried in cells that
are not allowed to
speak, the governors
that rule with lies and
death, and the sorrow
that sucks up the poor's
dreams.
no,
I am afraid of the
blindness, the faraway
freedom, the shameless
inequality, and the walls

with razors and nails
that sparkle in the sun
until America can no
longer speak!

Words

what more can I say about
the fool who lived in a Fifth
Avenue tower, the clowns
who parade around him in
the name of a white history
and the world that cries with
the eyes of migrant children?
what more can I say of the
contorting voices racially
dividing, the weak who suffer
wrong and the beating hearts
of mothers who scream for
dead kids? what can I tell you
about the boy holding a toddler
picture in front of him in a day-
long funeral march, the strings
that play in the pit and the satisfied
old men with power who look
away, content? when will you
chant for us "There is a balm in
Gilead and chariots to lead us
on home?"

El Norte

the caravan departs today
for the near uncrossable

border, the smell of sweet
fruit juices in the air on a

dim village street, chattering
mothers with infants in arms

debating what is right, youth
preparing to emerge from the

years of being buried beneath
English lies, and a local priest

on hand with a prayer to blow
the walkers clear of the words

from harsh white tongues. the
migrants in the greatest homeless

history told, the inheritors of the
earth who suffer poverty, endure

rape, experience hunger, grieve
death, flee violence, and are the

world's latest slaves rush to the
border in their Brown flesh to find a

place further than had ever been
imagined from home. they are on

the move with blistered feet toward
El Norte, that committed crimes for

more than a century on their Spanish-
speaking roads and sang of liberty,

equality, and freedom without a single
lick of shame.

Street Name

on Loisaida Avenue the
Caribbean island survivors

emerged from the ashes of
their nameless dead with

vivid memories of relatives,
friends, teachers, and priests

living in their hearts, born to
a world of madness, rejection,

seasonal joys, stumbling with
old junkies on the way to the

roof for a high, visiting funeral
homes close to the block with

dreadful tears for the latest kid
stripped of life in a country

of thinning freedom. we used to
call the street Avenue C until

Spanglish tongues took over, and
heaven threatened anyone who

denied a Puerto Rican presence on
lower Manhattan streets. the congas

now play in the park, cleansing whatever
tries to break these poor hearts, and the

sweet drumming in the neighborhood
declares Puerto Ricans will endure long

past the day history has a page written
for the last time about Nueva York.

The Walk

we could spend the time
walking First Avenue to

Chinatown talking at
the edges of unfamiliar

blocks and letting words
fall from our tongues

to bounce like a Spaulding
handball on the old city

sidewalk. we could pause
in front of the synagogue,

nestled on the bottom floor
of Tito's apartment building,

looking like a Pentecostal
storefront that is attended

by the owner of Moishe's
pastry shop, to ask for a

divine sign. maybe you
would prefer to walk hand-

in-hand without saying a
single word, smile at the

birds spying us from their
fire escape roosts, with

eyes open to people trying
to love themselves. the truth is

it doesn't matter what street
we take so long as the light

keeps playing with us and I can
share a thousand stories of

your beautiful look.

Never a Prayer

in the evening, when
the appetite of those

who have left the scent
of their blistered feet

on the road arises, the
newspapers are printing

the latest set of lies the
unrepentant asshole who

powders his nose with
the dust of our crushed

bones invents for citizens
hard of hearing. shadows

lean even in the dark to
say, "Sweet fools, you never

believed Mr. Orange skin,
with the hallelujah smile

and a bunch of bad dreams,
would make his bed in the

White House." when will
the lawmakers in Congress

say in unison, "The idiot
has gone too far?" when will

they admit seven deadly sins
are not enough to satisfy this

man, who relishes bringing a
nation to its knees? it appears

it will take more than God to
correct the thoughts escaping

the hole in the center of his
fat jowls! nevermind the

wait, instead let justice roll
out sentences and let jailers

toss away the key!

In These Times

on the steps of the
Lincoln Memorial
the marble from the great
monument reeked of sadness
given how far the nation has
strayed from its martyred first
Republican president. the pen that
made a people free, the dream
of equality uttered on its great
steps, the bitter strife of Martin
Luther King, and the shackles
stripped from our scarred wrists,
our history torn to shreds by the
rich man in the White House with
the pathetic presence of a president
who jails truth and defiles national
memory with a fat tongue uttering
daily filth. on the steps of the Lincoln
Memorial I wondered what would
Trump's white country do without
Black, Brown, Yellow and Red people
to beat and slay?

God Knows

they came a long way to
find unwelcoming white faces.

they prayed the whole walk with
devout tongues nailed in jails today.

they saw children lowered into
graves with tears and silence.

the butchers with rusty nails for
suits tossed hate at all of them. they

found a future full of harm in a
country whose president enjoys

his screwed-up sense of right in all
the places he settles down to eat.

they see churches can't live without
bodies but the good news goes to hell.

they wonder what is the point of
recollecting heaven on a star-spangled

choked earth.

The Methodists

the conference
brings delegates to
its days to deliberate
what we do and think
despite the hoarse tears
from those denied their
humanity by the tongues
too thick for God's words.
by the end of its sessions
love for some was cast aside,
the wounded body was mutely
unhealed and the weeping
began to creep across the world.
the conference pastors spent day after day
talking to God, dressing up goodness,
and handing out vague looks of love,
while wearing moth-eaten robes
to adorn their self-important figures
in God's magnificently flawed world.
the conference came to the hour of decision,
and in the name of the Mysterious,
who spreads her gracious wings for us,
voted to fall from Jacob's ladder,
pale with sadness, and splinter into ruins
our most beautiful rainbow.

Barrio Boy

you can see my toasted-brown
face any Sunday, burning church

incense on the steps of building
1203 like I did for martyrs far

from here with street kids who
never heard the wind cough up

English words, played for hours
on a dusty church field, and ,when

no one was looking, drank holy
water to quench thirst. when I

sit on the stoop in the moonlight
in poor clothes, the darkness finds

a way to creep over to mother me
and wait for the morning to happen

once again. when the foodstand
ladies come around with their carts

with crosses, charms, and Spanish-
speaking treats, the eyes on crisp

Brown faces swell, everyone feels
everlastingly at peace, and Mother Mary,

we know, fills us with dreams. when
I breath the incense, thinking about

the tiny apartment where we crowd
into a room to sleep with saints, recalling

the English lessons at Public School
66, my blistered heart says living here

molds stories like the wind blowing
across the vast brown earth.

Good Friday

Lord, occupy yourself with
broken hearts like in the first
light days, write on them the
way to your scented garden, let
us hold love in our hands
until lovers multiply in the
places beaten by stones and
permit us a place against your
shoulder to give thanks. Lord,
look for us in the crowds longing
for two fish and five loaves, in
the shade of day remind us of
the meaning of your Good
Friday, softly speak into our
ears about what happened before
our birth, guide us to put the
tender pages written about you
under our night pillows to find
our way to fresh worldly dreams,
wander with us the streets, across
the country borders and the closed
doors to knock. Lord, in a world treating
us like thieves, think of us kindly
and let us visit your elusive paradise
even for a thick hour.

The Bell Tower

I was breathing smoke-filled
air that trembled in my veins,
barely able to see the clouds
floating above the bell tower
in the lighted dark. the country
that once stamped herself free
fell that night into the arms of
the slavish flames that danced
an evil night away with the loud
screams of blasphemy. edgeless
gloom was reached like a call
for the first alphabet that gave us
the word that birthed this holy
church. though God too often
does not consider it necessary
to speak in the careless hours,
when Notre Dame burned on the
suffering surface of French earth
we demanded hidden love to offer
comforting words and delivery to
exquisite Christ-like peace.

Confess

in these
strange times
innocent flesh
cracks
with prayers
of distress
where the
long-severed
God dwells.
I must
confess
on the fresh
mound of tears
your eyes
can't see
light
is lessening
on all the
streets
for the Brown
kids who
have
hauled the
last supper
with mothers
since birth.
the longed-
for
things
are still
out of reach
and

raucously fleeing
our
sweet
dark skin
the history
of the
nation
gallops.

Dear Friends

I have been walking the streets,
listening to others talk about the

country under Trump's custody
for days on this side of the great

ocean, thinking about kids who
sleep beneath bridges, mothers

separated from infants who are
forever lost, the vigilant looking

over their shoulders, unable to
find a white-faced welcome and

the hundreds of reasons churches
offer for silence. I overheard a

group of American tourists on
las Ramblas speaking loosely

beneath hazy stars about the light
of liberty not shining on the dark-

skinned immigrants at home and
abroad. their words wounded my

aging Spanglish flesh and shouted
deep inside me, "Go back to wherever

you came from, spic." I sat down to
watch the world in faces walk past,

then concluded our names will escape
to the future and the stone-hearted

American tourists will choke one
day on their fucken contempt.

Postcards

the postcards fade in
boxes holding stories
of foreigners on Catalan
streets, the half-dressed
girls God feeds, and the
curling bay sailed by an
injurious admiral of a
world believed round.
the rushing dust makes
dim memories of them,
while the moonlight over
new world rooftops cannot
even offer a precious drop
of truth. will they harden
in the light, become quiet
faces for sleepless nights,
the shards of hearts in tiny
pieces begging for another
day? who would have said
five hundred years later you
would brush shoulders with
angels, strangers, vagabonds,
dreamers, and a simple Christ
with eyes still taking sides?
listen, when the lights of the
next year begin to break the
darkness, get the postcards
out to bless you in the holy
name of the maker of sweet
things.

Easter

I met them on the sidewalk
in the new day, carrying on

bent shoulders the weight
of a mocking border, giving

thanks for the crossing and
changing beneath Sunday's

tumbling clouds. we talked
into the late afternoon, their

voices sweeter than prayers
riding the sky like winged

angels, wondering on this
of all days when heaven will

do its part. they confessed on
the corner, where a confused

priest blasphemed Christ more
times than the old lady sitting

at her window could say in
defense of love, they had not

visited a flower-filled church
for months. we did not talk

about Easter egg hunts, pretty
church lilies, the hours with

bunnies on parade, instead we
talked about what happened to

Jesus, the crosses left in the
desert sand, the uncertain days

in America, and faith in God's
generous love. then, we quietly

cried.

Godless

the people across the border
carry pockets full of nails to

hammer into Brown feet on
Spanish-speaking soil. they

offer water in cups packed
with broken glass and push

us into cages in the name of
the Wall. they pray to a God

the poor cannot confess, the far-
off everlastingness they spend

lives to praise and that dark
need to call us the transporters

of violence, crime, rape, and
sin. with harsh English they

say, "Who asked you to come?"
and the faint limbs of children

beneath heaven above are mocked
by their cold hearts. someday

they will all learn to see that this
Pax Americana that pours around

the globe uses freedom on Capitol
Hill to slaughter, steal, and tighten

its yoke round dark captive nations
roofed by its shade. I wonder, will

the sacred few across the border
walk in the great dark with a slanted

light and hobble with us to the edge
of Eden to see us whole?

San Juan

on the streets of San Juan
they stroll, speaking English
fluently with Spanish tongues.
the colors on the walls like a
beggar slip into fading light
with the life that hobbles about
in this time after Hurricane Maria.
I can see the ocean that felt like home
to me when I lived on crying
streets, the faces of the old
men who were then just kids,
even hear the stories rolling
in like the waves, saying, "We
are citizens but never free."
I can taste the sugarcane
that comforted me in the
old plaza when my fourteen-
year-old veins screamed
Bronx Spanglish for a fix.
tomorrow I will visit the
cathedral to light candles,
take a knee, and plead for
my people who find life
in the very places America
only hates. Today, I give
thanks for seeing paradise
dance with palm trees!

The Apartment

behind the small apartment
blinds they sit to eat, talking

about the peculiar sounds of
English, the bare two-room

walls, and the ancient piety
stripped of familiar customs

in this country, calling women
and children a threat. on the

table, migrants afraid of being
seen placed a fresh stack of

pupusas and begin praying
loudly to their undocumented

God about their injuries, fears,
and the eucharist that melts in

their blue hearts. after a brief
silence, one old woman says

how effortlessly the country
that supported military rule,

thickening death, and crosses
for the poor forgets. I must

tell you of the weeping that
overwhelmed this mother's

chocolate face, and the room
that trembled with the sighs of

terrified migrants. I must tell
you they wondered what comes

next in this midway to nowhere
world, killing dreams with English

speeches and staggering white
hate.

The Vacant

we are scattered on this
land never convinced by

resurrection, recalling the
fallen in the bloody fields

of civil war, receiving spit
on our Brown faces and

weeping for the children
who are American born.

the pitiless days that aim to
undo hope in our new life

have an odor of death
about them, strongest

in the evening air, and
in apartments coughing

to find sleep. we have tried
for months to displace the

darkness, the tempest of
white nationalist hate and

the savagery of those in love
with cages of indefensible

sin. we light candles to
help make our way toward

the boundless treasures of life
and love that cannot be so far

from the slamming doors that
belong to these vacant people.

Idolatry

they no longer listen to
the words of prophesy that

helped them make a new
exodus to a land across the

sea which they stole from the
nations who suffered their

barbarous acts. they have not
perfected God's words, the

reconciling business of the
church, the building of a New

Jerusalem to gather the crucified
of the earth. they love to utter

dirty words, twist their failures
by the neck of dark bodies that

dangle from trees and relish
cutting the cords behind the

knees of those with nonwhite
skin. some among them say

the accidents of history will
give way in a split-second to

paradise near, approaching
with song and then to fully

rest on weary heads—in the
unkind time of the *barrio,*

where they toss the remains
of sacrificed lives even the

children wonder!

The Other Stars

in the wounded night, with
angels tied by the guilty to

sickly trees in the city, migrants
roam in search of their Spanish-

speaking villages, the false
witnesses master hate, leaving

church early. the old religion
does not mention death in the

alleys, wire cages, private jails,
the border crossing, wet thorns

pushed into soft hearts, and in
the places marked by crosses

on our grieving maps. the lovers
of whiteness who sip poison and

sit silently as two-faced politicians
convict Christ in strangers, will one

day lay unburied with their crimes
disclosed by huge banners to the

pitiless side of God's earth. under
the stars, with wrinkled photos,

the hurting beg heaven once again
to return the sweet feeling of rest

in this land of extra shadows and
pale shaved heads until the dark-

faced Jesus comes to open wicked
doors.

Midnight

I see them in the restless
nights of Spring when the

air cools from the playful
voices of children coping

with the strange speeches
delivered about them that

are not sweet. I find them
sitting on the steps of the

empty churches letting love
run like water through a

filter and remaining savagely
quiet in the cruelest months

of the lost nation. I see the
newspapers from the trash

heaps at the corner of the lot
with rowed cages containing

stories masquerading as
truth, light creeping about

the shadows and pictures of
faces full of ignorance, so

untroubled by injustice. I see
the authorities have stripped

guiltless families of names,
numbered them in English,

and declared the lot unworthy
of liberty and God. I see

them trembling in the open
in a world where the least of

these are neither reverenced nor
cherished despite divinity

standing in their midst. I
noticed when the children

die in false arrests,` well-lit
big churches competing for

members are never there to
call it abomination and say

kind prayers.

Prayer

tell me, spirit who listens to
prayer, do the words coming

from my lips make sense?
when the night is too long

for the nearing light will you
bring it to me? tell me, when

the looming judgment day
makes its way into these parts,

will America take a knee in
shame on seeing a Black

God? tell me, spirit, do you
see the trees with lynching

rope, the slavery yet in our
ancient souls, and the weak

voices trying to get past the
stars to fall gently on your

divine ears? tell me, spirit,
did you see the Black boy

beaten to the ground then
shot, the migrant infant who

last night drowned in a river
crossing, the Brown mother

with teeth kicked out, and
the sighing faces so full of

grief? tell me, spirit, why do
you tolerate fancy churches

inoculating people with fear,
ignorance, and hate in the

name of stone idols and a
double-faced, white God?

I will keep praying since you
still haunt my dreams, but will

not use clever English words
to help you understand the

horrors.

Waiting

I cannot explain the years
roiled in history near and
far, the love carried inside
these veins in the middle of
a civil war, how long nights
were bent by your scent as
America boiled, the joyous
sanity of walking up the side
of mountains, roaming open
markets, lighting candles to
split the air, and peeling my
eyes when you gave birth to
lives destined for heaven. I
cannot explain why the time
of suffocating dust could not
settle inside of me when I felt
you closer than my soul and
like an endless light startling
shadows. I cannot explain the
singing on the other side of
the river, my love, but when
eternity claims me from this
short life with a final breath
I promise never to stop drifting
with the earthly winds looking
for you.

The American Way

one night they gathered to
begin the trip across the

borders of three countries
sin papeles to the republic

that confuses any Spanish
speaker for Mexican. they

joked about taking young
children in their *mochilas,*

with their little heads out
for air to breathe some of the

American Dream, on the long
walk before reaching the land

that will call them "illegals"
with a government that labels

Hispanics, people of color,
wetbacks, criminals, and spics.

they all climbed into a van
pointing north, offered prayers

to the God of the poor, and
made the sign of the cross on

their foreheads, then whispered
in the night, "Heaven does not

require English and brand names
are for burning." it was quiet for

the next 20 kilometers when a
teen boy turned to the driver to

say in America they talk about
Christ in big stadiums, make him

a monster full of hideous hate for
people like us, and call their science

fiction about the creator of life
the great American way. then,

a ten-year-old girl added we learned
holy things superior to that stupid

idea of God!

Cross the River

in the ordinary time
the search for magic

moments is with us
on the streets, choked

by Spanish speakers
living day to day inside

the insistent argument
made up by those with

a few more years of life
in this occupied country

who say, "Get out." we are
not confused about how

hard hate works looking
for us, always covered up

in newspapers and blown
over on windy nights to the

parts of the city strange to
the deliberately ignorant

white folk downtown who
regularly slip away from it

all in evening suppers. the
day the pigeons formed a

swarm on the rooftop of the
old building where little Ana

lives, I was certain it was a
sign the block would start

speaking in the language the
Pentecostals call tongues, and

the Salvadoran girls, tending to
the rich white kids down York

Avenue, would touch us, breaking
out in song about secrets known

to the distant stars and days
of degradation, along with

the harassing law, would finally
meet their fucken end.

Sunrise

at the first light of day
I love to sit in the candle-
lit sanctuary, listening
to the bells ring awake the
neighborhood with songs
that make their way like
a bird in flight to the tent
village at the little creek.
I have never imagined a
day beginning without the
bells that keep us glad and
echo in the Bronx cemetery,
slowly raising the dead. when
night comes down the people
on the block say the church
here is poor like them and
always the best place to spend
long hours noticing darkness
chased downtown.

Neca

it was the late winter, when
the sky overhead was playful

blue, that you called from the
hospital with news of a tumor

that took sight from one eye
before being removed—we

cried. sister, we talk at the
end of each day when you

are finished, you lean back
on the bed tilting your head

for the eye that takes up the
task of sight and talk about

the apartments disappeared
on the block but never in us

erased. we wait now for what
may come, still counting the

blessings to be said, smiling
about the curly hair that falls

from your head, and sixty-one
years of dearest life. I will

sail with you down the East
River, reminding you of the

names of the mural painters
from the neighborhood, the

nightclub where you danced
your first salsa steps with a

brother who already left this
world, and, when passing the

big old church, declaring the
new life that will arrive on

faith from far away. sister,
when the silence spreads out

I will do my best to find you
in the blood, bone, and fragile

life forever breaking into the
light.

Weep

Jesus
is not
your
white man
like the Bible
stories you feed
us.
like us,
this refugee
Jew
met death on
a tree.
Jesus is not
your white man
full of hate,
He
was never
dreamed by
Europe
in
beautiful
Black skin
though
from
Calvary
He
reached out
to make
divine
dark
people
like me.

Jesus is not your
white man
in a world
without
end,
He knows
the lashes in
my
Black soul,
the thousands
of ways we are
beaten and
betrayed,
and
He
sees the
satisfied
houses
untouched
by shame.
Jesus is not
your
white man
the
Bible says
so.

The Republic

"We the
people"
it says in
the founding
document
of
the Republic
that never kept
Black bodies
from auction
and
punished us
for the
transgression
of dark
skin.
we are
here,
citizens
no less,
in spite
of
those
who won't
hold our
calloused
hands.
"We the
people,"
so it says,
with church
bells
ringing

and
Whitman
in the
wind
declaring
the beauty of
democracy,
the piloting
of rivers
unaided by stars
and
stories of
belonging
that speak
of people
not white.
we the people,
from North, South,
East, and West,
awake from
centuries
of
filthy dreams,
hold on
to
the tempest-tossed,
and
let
this land
be made
for
any
magnificently
free!

Carmen Julia

today I saw Carmen Julia
with her mother on the way
to the shops on the boulevard
for a last walk. they held each
other's hands like they were on
their way to a Sunday church
service, her mother for years
well-practiced in giving her
daughter warmth and smiling
at all the children on the block
at play. they walked by me like
two Puerto Rican girls on their
way to search for living water
in the little park with the Army
recruiting station, where *el Viejo*,
who spent days pleading for change,
could give directions and explain
where to turn. no one imagined
the darkness piercing the whole
neighborhood of Spanish-speaking
hearts, the fragrance made by the
flowers planted in perfect pots at
the church not reaching us, and
her mother delivered by the thief
who took her daughter's life to a
world of sorrow. Carmen Julia
was buried in a Bronx cemetery
and her mother who has grown
old with tears still walks the
streets, holding her hand.

Favored

we cling each day to
life that, like a corpse

tied to a MAGA
pick-up truck, is

dragged around all
night. no one has yet

dared to put a stop to
it since it's not white

bodies made of flesh
and blood paraded on

the streets. when God
examines the evidence,

not counting the utter
acts of ignorance, what

will be left standing of
these vulgar citizens for

the last judgment? the
mechanisms of justice

break into pieces and the
men of government are

secure in their tearless
houses of filth. our

broken, Brown bodies
that scream louder than

war, the white violence
that makes our children

bleed, and the frightening
days of horror experienced

in the name of a Jim Crow
God, we believe one day

will perish in flames to make
way for our days of mourning

to end with a great banquet!

Madness

the madman is up in the
early morning hours, writing
sour notes from his vacuous
dark self, looking over the
papers for stories of praise,
his heart not shedding a tear
for the forgotten whose blood
stains his hands. the madman is
sitting in his room drunk on
the cruelty that burns in his
veins, imagining a thousand
more ways to dirty the world
with hellish follies, aiming to
loot the nation of its worth,
and belching more lies about
God on his side. the madman
rejects reason like a disease,
makes criminals judges of
law, desecrates the sacred by
poisoning the earth, fornicates
himself in the White House
dark, and is determined to
solicit more followers to lead
the world to greater unsaintly
days. the madman is full of
sin, like that eating the flesh of
the innocent, and on the bodies
hanging until death that God,
the Bible says, made equal by
blood.

Subway Station

the morning voices at the
subway station don't speak

English and the horn puffing
away on the platform sings in

the same Spanish of the
girls on the station floor,

kicking a crumpled cup around
with party dress shoes. for now,

time is unable to reach the
breathing lungs, swooping

sparrows, and Puerto Rican
kids changing like characters

in a story. silence in between
loud voices must surely be the

place where the angels gather
to discuss the signs of the cross,

where to find the New Jerusalem
on Simpson Street, and why the

Hoe Avenue church, untouched
when the Bronx burned, locks its

doors. we may ride the tracks
across two boroughs to the last

stop of the number two train going
south just to hear the grinding of

old subway breaks and see with
our own eyes where god was left

behind.

Forty-Five

wicked
cruel
incompetent
illogical
daft
ignorant
unethical
criminal
lawless
impulsive
infantile
corrupt
hateful
racist
misogynistic
homophobic
xenophobic
nationalist
egotistical
narcissistic
idiot
arrogant
toxic
liar
fraud
dishonest
disgusting
annoying
clown
bully
rapist
divisive

disloyal
unqualified
asshole
IMPEACHABLE!!!!!

Little Sister

you asked me not to weep
on these bright days when

life still moves and prays in
your sickened limbs. I do my best,

siting in the churchyard mornings,
remembering how you ran about

school grounds when a little girl
without care and a stranger to the

tears you now spill when no one is
looking for God to finally release

you from pain. I believe, dear little
sister, you will rest in the bosom of

Jesus, find you are finally at home,
and look down at us, the broken-

hearted. I will do my best to listen
for the sound of your voice in the

wind telling me the good Lord has
taken your hand, wiped away the

tears, and cradled you with love
in his arms, just like the lessons

Sister Jane Carmel taught us one
long summer in the Bronx. I will

never think of you as gone when that
dreaded day takes us to the wilderness

to read once again Psalms of
lament. before your broken body

separates us in time forever I must
declare, dear little sister, I love you,

and I will find you like a lost gift
one day at the pearly gates.

Speechless

sitting on the stoop one
morning, I was still in the

morning light, observing birds
above my head in soundless

flight, the bandaged Puerto
Ricans heading downtown

for cheap work, a window
half opened from which news

escaped that was played on a
radio, broadcasting the devil

that is in the old president's mind,
feeding it lies and a whole lot

of hell to call paradise. little
children began to walk the

sidewalk, trying to skip over
cracks, their poverty on this

side of the world terrifying
to God, who for some reason

hides in the neighborhood in
aging widows' dreams. Jesus

of Nazareth, with bleeding hands
and feet, walked across the street

though no one would admit it
in the pretty big churches and

packaged American world of
pocket spirituality. a thousand

words of Spanish turned in my
head and my public school

English was tongue-tied and
left thoroughly speechless as

I waited for a divine sign to
show up on the block.

Brittle

where is God in the city
churches, on the border,
the workplace raid, the
children scared, the locked
cages, the long walk North,
and the cold nights forced
to sleep beneath a bridge? I
have a mouthful of prayers
given to me after they crossed
the border with the falsely accused
that I was charged to deliver to
the houses of God damaged by
duplicity and unable to speak
Spanish. the words have left a
hole in my skull that you can
clearly see, they keep me awake
at night thinking of the pieces of
Brown lives exhausted in a white
wilderness and I wonder when
the good book will perfectly undo
the toxicity of a culture that cannot
imagine how the holy verses now
bleed.

Crossing

I waited for the news to ring
over the telephone, staring at

the first names of some of the civil
war dead with my lonely God in

the country of hardship, coughing
softly in a corner of the study next

to the moaning clock. the ache
in my stomach that began in the

sanctuary, with hundreds of dead
voices taking turns speaking through

dancing flames on the candles
before the Mother of Peace, grew

more intense by the hour. the call
would be proof to me that the Lord

could still pull splinters from crying
tongues, carry you across the lethal

waters of a river and let you take a
deep breath on the other side of the

border, safe. whatever thanks was
being made that season in homes, I

dreamed of roasting corn and holding
you in that bright starry night. now,

in America, you walk among the
English-speaking people who seldom

recall dreams giving the good Lord
thanks!

Near

the world goes on with
clouds moving across
the sky, the landscape
in change, stones on
the mountain paths, in
deep rivers, and beside
the ancient trees worn
by time. before we turn
into memories, someone
will say we lived in the
long, insufferable days of
an unwelcoming nation,
lifted children in our arms
with a love that will burn
longer than any star gazing
down upon this country
of money. in this mysterious
sigh before the silence of eternity,
what matters are the sparkling
dreams bright in the eyes of
our beautiful, dark-skinned
kids.

Loosened

here
in this
created world,
with bodies
commanded
by God
to cross every
border,
we are more
united
by acts
dispensing
far more
cruelty
than love.
the earth,
trembling
before the
mighty power
of God,
cannot make
us stop
and
the days
ahead
ignored will
see us
united
once again
weeping
around
our blazing

homes.
here,
in day
and
night,
pray love
does
not
take
permanent
flight.

The Cross

where has the fearless
commitment to justice
gone, the sense of horror
for the Central American
kids immigration detention has
killed, the outrage that lifts
its voice against the decent
folk tolerant of their government's
inhumanity, the belief in a God
of life that condemns the hearts
bloated by a necro-politics that
leaves the world with sin and
the pious certain there is no
time of reckoning? why is evil
triumphant like some great
cause? why are the vulnerable groped
by filthy politicians, and the
innocent pounded by an obese
president into dust? will you be
there when he crucifies the Lord
in the detention camps for the
delight of heretics who bleed
the innocent, who oppose hate
for the sake of liberty for the
captives? will the ugly speeches
ever end, the white hoods get
ripped to threads, and the country
dream in every color and speak
in all its tongues? "Justice matters,"
say the meek, and it should roll
across the landscape in the name
of human decency and the cross
of Calvary from which another
world comes!

Naked World

the night that appears
behind the building on

West Farms Road can
be seen from the street

that runs all the way to
the East River where the

fishing boats never hired
by the kids on the block

are docked. the remains
of fallen buildings in the

neighborhood tremble in
the lone darkness, and heaven

shed tears for them long
before Tita, who sang holy

hymns to her disabled daughter
like lullabies, moved to another

distant block. at the river edge
we remembered why we came

to this naked world, beyond
the reach of any promised

saintly hour, how very well
practiced we are, waiting to

be set free and become experts
at shouting in piously flawed

churches, "God is too far away
from these fucken streets to

see." we vow to make your
walls pitiably useless and to

keep Spanish words leaping
on the streets for the people

with cruelty smeared on their
pasty faces.

The Darkening

I count the minutes,
battered by the bald-
faced political lies
giving shape to the
hideous events that
erase humanity from
us. I sit silently with
an avalanche of fresh
questions meandering
in the hollows of my
broken heart for the
people who find the
dark precious with
the company of a God
who never accepts the
injustices done to them.
I pray louder than the
shouting graves for the
savage old Klansmen
in legislators' clothes
stomping on the bodies
of the innocent in all the
places engineered in the
name of history's fallen
and disappeared. what
is the good news? when
will we see it?

Father

father, you slipped into the
long sleep several years ago,

following your first-born who
left this world before his time,

into the silence, only weighed
down by that stone heart you

dragged for years. I have one
picture of you in an old box

wearing a tuxedo surrounded
by faces I do not recognize, save

the young Puerto Rican girl not
wearing a smile beside you who

gave me life. I hardly recall the
sound of your voice, the lines on

your Brown face, the first English
words you ever spoke, the hollering

you were fond of when home for
a few days in the cracked skin of

a drunken sailor. I do remember, now
that you have slipped into an eternal

slumber, the unforgiving beatings you
gave my mother, the mouthful of words

you spat like nails into my ear on a
Bronx corner across the street from

an abandoned building where your
oldest son was slowing killing himself

with dope, and the countless excuses
you had for failing at fatherhood. I

suspect wherever you are there is a
truth thicker than you ever imagined

on this side of the grave, a story that
keeps coming back like Sisyphus with

the boulder to torment your feverish
eternity of penance. I bet you hear

voices shouting, "You cannot wake to
experience what you never cared to

know." when you weren't looking, I
turned away from your Nowhere land,

rose from a junkie grave, and leaned
into the fresh air my own children led

me to breathe.

Suffering

you know
the face
of
God
and how
it showed
suffering
like
the martyrs
back
home.
now,
in the
loudly
crying darkness,
the
speechless
nights of
hell,
the broken
dreams
in cages,
the
suffering servant,
impaled by
their
offenses,
hides
to strengthen
you with
love.

Little Bird

I watched
a
little bird,
pushed gently
by the
wind,
bounce
on dry
leaves
behind
green
bushes.
in its
tiny eyes
there was
a lingering
need
to find
a way
to
the habits
of flight
performed
by
a mother
nearby.
I confess
the tiny
creature
dancing
around
my feet,

along with
the
many feathered
voices
swooping
above
its near
bald head,
moved me
to imagine
the trees'
branches,
a place
of rest
from which
a rushing
world
might
stop
for a
moment
to listen
to songs
overspill
walls
and
moats
to enter
all
the
upset
places.

When

when did they look away
from these children born

into the violence that makes
a spectacle of the new and

phony White House? when
will they see God in faces

drowned in the river, the
cages guarded by patriotic

pedophiles, the fathers who
hang themselves in cells,

despairing mothers weighed
down by rape, and thousands

of bodies detained in Brown
broken flesh? the traveling

hours of such cruel days linger
unkindly in us, candle wicks

burn into darkness, and heaven
on earth remains silent. when

will the houses of prayer find
divine words to put a stop to

it and confess the sin in this
sadistic time that haughtily

returns Christ's gift? we say,
with such near-perfect silence,

"These Americanos will wake
one day, exposed for having

faith in nothing!"

Mentiras

you were only six when
the lights were darkened
in the bedroom by one of
your older brothers to hear
a scary story he carried back
from the Boys' Club Camp
so full of trees. the haunting
sounds that came out of him
still make you shiver at your
age when the lights are real
low and a strong wind howls
outside. the saints on your
mother's altar where you hid
for cover received your panting
breath like prayer and finally
I found you in the shadows
to say, "Nequita, don't worry, it's
just a story invented from big
old lies!" sometimes when it feels
like it's darker, you find ways to
show light, to let it reach down
the saddest lanes and press its
way through the cloudy night
to distant heaven—my little
sister, so acquainted with hard
times, you blossomed strangely
with little water to make the
shuttling days smell always
like Spring.

Migrant

the long walk from the village
felt like it would never come to

an end. he crammed a portion
of the best times to carry with

him, stories worth telling in an
alien place and a world possessed

by others who do not speak in
Spanish sentences. he will live

somewhere in New York, near
the street corner photographed

in the magazine, buried among
his things, even make friends

with other people who learned
to be faceless in the dark, and

exist for a very long time in the
spaces between dreams. in time

he will find a job packing boxes,
washing dishes, cleaning offices,

unpacking produce, cooking at a
grill, bussing tables, painting the

halls of tenements, looking at the
citizens who possess a life he does

not know. his starved eyes will
long to see the tiny village in the

valley, his body will desire to feel
the wind that knows him by name,

and sitting drowsily on the urban
stoop, will find him longing to run in

the corn fields beneath the hot
tropical sun. when the wet slush

of winter rolls in he will decry the
cold that almost makes him forget

why he came.

Politics

what politics can make me

look away from the Spanish

chatting voices that speak the

frightening truths others will

not name? how can I agree with

the two-faced politicians, blessed

by the ministers of their lily-

white Christ? who sings down

the Lord's chariots for the kids

without freedom, equality tossed

to hell, Brown people moaning

like slaves, and America flying

a flag of shame?

Morning

it is another morning waiting patiently to be opened once again with the school janitor's bunch of keys, the light widening on the streets will disclose the corner where the 41st precinct cop yelled at the shoeshine boys saying he was going to arrest the "bunch of you spics" cause Papo was drinking Colt 45 on the job. bells begin to sound on the sidewalk from the neighborhood church in the distance, ordering time to float over the rooftops, the mourning widows, and the migrants seeking refuge. on the beautifully colored streets the food carts with concoctions made by Brown *abuelita* hands are setting up like Southern Boulevard was just another piece of Mesoamerica in an English-speaking city bursting with defiant accents. yes, it is another morning and not one pliant word will gush from our formerly enslaved lips!

The Cry

what do you think of the history
that suffers on the border, in the
camps, and the fields still soaked
with the blood of the frail bodies
you made, God? when you lose the
life of another Mesoamerican child,
does a spirit haunt you in the great
unknown, Lord? when you look into
the skeletal faces gruesomely slanted
in America's pale light do you feel
empty in your heavenly throne? when
will you visit the mournful hearts to
give comfort, the teen girls forced to
wear period-stained clothes, the Brown-
faced people with blistered, unwashed
feet, the fathers about to hang themselves
in cells, and the mothers who never forgot
you in prayer, God? what will it take for
you to stop them from lengthening time
until we have all disappeared? when you
hear our shrieks tonight, hurry to tell the
architects of holocausts and these modern
detention cages they are so far from you,
God!

The Anniversary

on this day the sun will
circle us once again to
warm the altering world,
just like that first September.
we begn writing lines for the
sake of love. whatever this
thing is that aligned us closely
for years, shaped a way to see
the world, disabled errors with
the ancient kiss, shouted joyfully
for the blessing of kids, I say it
is a world without end. in the
autumn evening, with you, I will
give thanks for the certainty that
when the Holy Ghost shows up to
set me on a new journey, I will
walk through all of our secret
passages, declaring passionately
once more, "Nothing in the world
can separate us!" it took a little
time for me to realize stars burn
for you at night and the flowers
where the hummingbirds feed
open to the sound of your calling
voice. why would I ever want to
travel beyond this gentle moment
in time permitted to me?

www.ingramcontent.com/pod-product-compliance
Lightning Source LLC
Chambersburg PA
CBHW071621170426
43195CB00038B/1739